The Panic Attack Workbook

A Workbook of Therapeutic Assignments

Between Sessions Resources

Norwalk, CT

The Panic Attack Workbook
By Lawrence E. Shapiro, PhD

Cover by Mike Canavan

Disclaimer: This book is intended to be used as an adjunct to psychotherapy. If you are experiencing serious symptoms or problems in your life, you should seek the help of an experienced mental health professional.

ISBN: 978-1-947009-00-4

Published by
Between Sessions Resources
304 Main Ave, #333
Norwalk, CT 06851

About the Author

Lawrence E. Shapiro, Ph.D., is a prolific author of self-help books and the inventor of more than 100 therapeutic games. Dr. Shapiro is known for his practical approach to helping others. He has written workbooks, storybooks, card games, board games, and smartphone apps. His interest and expertise cover a broad range of issues, from providing parents with lifesaving information in *The Baby Emergency Handbook* to reducing the incidence of suicide in the military with the award-winning app *Operation Reach Out*. His work has been translated into 29 languages.

About the Series

Between Sessions Resources publishes a variety of worksheets and other tools which are designed to be used as therapeutic homework. The Panic Attack Workbook is one of a series of assignment workbooks designed to help people practice the psychological skills they learn in therapy.

Table of Contents

Introduction   i

Understanding Your Panic Attacks   1

Rating Your Panic Attack Symptoms   4

Your Daily Mood Record for Overcoming Panic Attacks*   8

Calming Your Body with Progressive Muscle Relaxation*   9

Keeping Track of Your Relaxation Practice   10

The Grounding Technique*   11

Recording Your Use of the Grounding Technique   13

Becoming Aware of Your Upsetting Thoughts and Feelings   14

Tolerating Your Distressing Thoughts & Feelings with Mindfulness   17

Tolerating the Physical Discomfort from Your Anxiety   19

Recreating Your Physical Discomfort   20

Practicing Being Physically Uncomfortable   21

Stop Avoiding Situations that Make You Anxious   22

What Are the Odds?   23

Talking Back to the Thoughts that Make You Anxious   25

Using Coping Statements to Deal with Your Panic Attacks   33

Examining Your Success at Using Coping Statements   34

Controlling Your Anxiety with a "Worry Script"   35

Practicing Getting Anxious   38

Eliminating Unhelpful Coping Strategies   41

Creating an Exposure Hierarchy to Overcome Your Fears   43

Situations That Trigger Your Fear and Anxiety   45

Prioritizing the Situations that Trigger Your Fear/Anxiety   46

Practicing Exposure Therapy   47

Overcoming Setbacks in Overcoming Your Panic Attacks   48

Getting More Sleep Can Help Reduce Your Anxiety   51

Overcoming Anxiety with the Help of Exercise   53

How Diet Affects Your Mood   56

Building Your Support System to Overcome Your Anxiety   58

What Has Helped You?   62

Notes   64

*These worksheets have links to audio or video tools

The Panic Attack Workbook
Introduction

It's Time to Get Rid of Your Panic Attacks

If you have panic attacks, whether they occur every day or just occasionally, you should know that you can get rid of them forever. Panic attacks are considered to be one of the most treatable of all mental-health problems and, in most cases, you can learn the skills to get rid of your panic attacks in three to four months or 12 to 16 therapy sessions.

This workbook is designed to accompany treatment by a professional therapist trained to work with anxiety disorders. If you have purchased this book and do not presently have a therapist, you will certainly find the exercises in this book to be helpful; however, we do recommend that you work with a therapist. The treatment of panic attacks is typically not a straight road, so having a trained professional to guide you will make your journey to a panic-free life more direct.

Another reason that we recommend you seeing a therapist is that panic attacks can be confused with other conditions. A trained therapist will consider your history of panic attacks as well as other problems you may be having, such as depression, other anxiety disorders, or drug and alcohol abuse. Your therapist may also recommend a physical exam to rule out a thyroid condition, caffeine addiction, or certain medical problems that can cause people to have symptoms similar to those that occur with panic attacks.

What Are Panic Attacks?

A panic attack is a sudden episode of intense fear that triggers a severe physical reaction even though there is no real danger. Panic attacks can be very frightening. When panic attacks occur, you might think you're losing control, having a heart attack, or even dying.

Many people have just one or two panic attacks in their lifetimes, and then the problem goes away. But if you've had recurrent and unexpected panic attacks and spent long periods in constant fear of another attack, you may have a condition called panic disorder.

Experiencing recurring panic attacks is a serious problem, and just avoiding the panic attacks can make the problem worse. The severity of your problem will also depend on how much you worry in between your attacks and if you are constantly concerned about the possibility of having another panic attack.

This worry and fear of having a panic attack likely interferes with your daily functioning. The fear of panic attacks can lead people to change jobs, spend less time in the pursuit of leisure activities, avoid travel, and even skip important family celebrations. When you have a panic attack, you typically have a sense that something terrible is going to happen and your body responds with an automatic fear reaction. Your heart pounds in your chest, you may sweat, you may feel dizzy, you may even feel like you are going crazy. This attack can last up to an hour, although most people report that the intense panic reaction lasts from 10 to 15 minutes. Not surprisingly, people who restrict their lives because of a fear of having panic attacks will often develop symptoms of depression.

About one in three people with a panic disorder develops agoraphobia, a psychological condition defined as the fear of being in a place where you might experience a panic attack and not be able to find help or easily escape. People with agoraphobia are constantly on guard and typically restrict their world to avoid panic attacks. Some people develop a fixed route or only go to a confined territory where they feel safe. Many people with agoraphobia find it impossible to travel outside of their safety zones. In severe cases, people with agoraphobia won't even leave the house. Panic attacks may also be associated with other fears, such as claustrophobia or acrophobia (a fear of heights).

Many people have panic attacks without having a true panic disorder. When someone has a single panic attack, it does not mean they have a panic disorder. To get a diagnosis of a panic disorder, you must have had repeated panic attacks, they must be uncontrolled, and they must occur in various environments. People with a panic disorder may have had panic attacks seemingly out of the blue, when there was no obvious trigger present.

Will Medication Help You Overcome Your Panic Attacks?
Some people choose to take medication to help get over their panic attacks. This can be a good idea for some, but not for everyone. Medication can help you cope with the immediate or intense symptoms of anxiety, but you will still need to learn the psychological skills covered in this workbook to permanently overcome your panic attacks. It is important to note that all medications may have side effects and that some medications commonly used to treat anxiety disorders can be very addictive. You should discuss the pros and cons of using medication to help with your panic attacks with your therapist, as well as a medical doctor.

How to Use this Workbook
This workbook consists of 30 therapeutic homework assignments which will help you develop the psychological skills and behavioral patterns that will rid you of your panic attacks. Typically, a therapist will explain why each skill is important and demonstrate how it can best be learned. But the only way you can effectively reduce your fears and anxiety is to work on this problem between sessions. Practicing these skills is essential to successful treatment.

Several of the activities in this workbook have links to multimedia tools, both audio and video. The activities are indicated by an asterisk in the title, and these tools can help enhance your learning of new skills.

There are six sections of worksheets, and each section will help you learn a specific set of skills. Your therapist may assign these skills in order or he/she may pick and choose assignments from different sections to fit your specific needs and progress. The six sections include:

Understanding Panic Attacks
This section will help you assess the nature of your panic attacks and guide you to the appropriate level of help to achieve a more fulfilling life without needless worry and anxiety.

Learning to Calm Your Mind and Body
This section will teach you how to calm yourself when you feel anxious and out of control. The exercises will not only help you overcome your panic attacks but will help you whenever you feel anxious or stressed.

Tolerating Anxiety and Discomfort
The exercises in this section are pivotal to overcoming your fear of having a panic attack. They will help you understand that avoiding difficult feelings is never the answer, but rather, you must learn to tolerate the thoughts, feelings, and body sensations that trigger you distress.

Replacing Your Fears with Rational Thinking
As with all anxiety disorders, irrational thoughts about having panic attacks make it difficult to act in logical ways. The exercises in this section will teach you to recognize the automatic thoughts that are contributing to your anxiety and fears.

Changing Your Behavior and Facing Your Fears
You'll know that you have made a major change in your life when you learn to face the things that you fear, including tolerating the symptoms associated with your panic attack. This process is typically referred to as "exposure therapy" because you gradually expose yourself to the things you fear most.

Working towards a Permanent Change
In this section, you will learn how to prevent and manage a relapse. There are also activities to help you develop lifestyle habits that can literally change the biochemistry of your brain, reducing your vulnerability to stress and worry. The final assignment in the workbook will help you think back on what has helped you achieve your goal of living a panic-free life.

We hope you find this workbook to be beneficial in conquering your panic attacks. We congratulate you on your courage and determination to conquer your problem. For additional resources and to understand more about anxiety disorders, we encourage you to go to the website of the Anxiety and Depression Association of America at: www.adaa.org.

Understanding Your Panic Attacks

The more you understand about your panic attacks the closer you will be to getting rid of them for good. This worksheet is designed to give you an overview of your panic attacks and how they fit into the rest of your life.

How often do your panic attacks occur?   _____

How long do the panic attacks usually last?   _____

Below is a list of common symptoms of panic attacks. Rate the severity of each symptom on a scale of one to ten, where 1 = I do not have this symptom at all, and 10 = I have this symptom intensely.

_____ Palpitations, pounding heart, or accelerated heart rate

_____ Sweating

_____ Trembling or shaking

_____ Sensations of shortness of breath or smothering

_____ Feelings of choking

_____ Chest pain or discomfort

_____ Nausea or abdominal pain

_____ Feeling dizzy, unsteady, light-headed, or faint

_____ Chills or heat sensations

_____ Numbness or tingling sensations (paresthesia)

_____ Feelings of unreality or that you are going crazy

_____ Feelings that you are detached from yourself (depersonalization)

_____ Fear of losing control

_____ Fear of having a heart attack or dying

Note: The definition of a panic attack is the abrupt onset of intense fear or discomfort that reaches a peak within minutes and includes at least four of the above symptoms.

Answer Yes or No to the following questions:

_____ Do you experience a fear of places or situations where getting help or escape might be difficult, such as in a crowd or on a bridge?

_____ Do you feel unable to travel without a companion?

_____ For at least one month following an attack, have you felt persistent concern about having another one?

_____ For at least one month following an attack, have you worried about having a heart attack or "going crazy?"

_____ For at least one month following an attack, have you changed your behavior to try to avoid another panic attack?

_____ In addition to your panic attacks have you had other problems like changes in sleeping or eating habits?

_____ Do you feel sad or depressed more days than not?

_____ Do you feel disinterested in life more days than not?

_____ Do you feel worthless or guilty more days than not?

_____ During the last year, has the use of alcohol or drugs resulted in your failure to fulfill responsibilities at work, at school, or with your family?

_____ During the last year, has the use of alcohol or drugs placed you in a dangerous situation, such as driving a car, or gotten you arrested?

_____ During the last year, has the use of alcohol or drugs continued despite causing problems for you or your loved ones?

Describe your typical panic attack.

_____

_____

_____

_____

_____

What usually helps your panic attacks go away?

_____

_____

_____

_____

How would you say that your panic attacks affect your quality of life? In other words, how do your panic attacks keep you from living life to its fullest?

_____

_____

_____

_____

_____

How will your life change when you no longer have panic attacks?

_____

_____

_____

_____

_____

List any ongoing medical conditions and the current medications you are taking (including vitamins and supplements).

Medical Conditions	Medications
_____	_____
_____	_____
_____	_____
_____	_____
_____	_____
_____	_____

Rating Your Panic Attack Symptoms

Below is a list of common symptoms of a panic attack. Rate the severity each on a scale of one to seven, where 1 = I do not have this symptom at all, and 7 = I have this symptom intensely. Put a mark on the each scale that best describes the severity of this symptom when you have a typical panic attack.

Today's date: _____

Racing heart

1_____2_____3_____4_____5_____6_____7

Heart palpitations

1_____2_____3_____4_____5_____6_____7

Chest pain or discomfort

1_____2_____3_____4_____5_____6_____7

Difficulty breathing

1_____2_____3_____4_____5_____6_____7

Vision problems

1_____2_____3_____4_____5_____6_____7

Nausea

1_____2_____3_____4_____5_____6_____7

Shaking

1_____2_____3_____4_____5_____6_____7

Sweating

1   2   3   4   5   6   7

Dizziness

1   2   3   4   5   6   7

Numbness/tingling

1   2   3   4   5   6   7

Feeling like you are going to die

1   2   3   4   5   6   7

Other symptoms (Describe)_____

1   2   3   4   5   6   7

Other symptoms (Describe)_____

1   2   3   4   5   6   7

Other symptoms (Describe)_____

1   2   3   4   5   6   7

Other symptoms (Describe)_____

1   2   3   4   5   6   7

Panic Attack Log

Use this worksheet to record each attack. Complete this form for each attack *as it occurs.*

Date	Level*	Time Began	Time Ended	Symptoms	Type**	Where Are You?	What Are You Doing?	Are You Alone?	Thoughts before the Attack

* *Rate your level of panic on a scale of 0 to 10, where 0 means no panic, and 10 means the worst panic possible.*

** *There are three types of attacks: Spontaneous (S), which appear to come out of nowhere; Anticipatory (A), which occur while you are thinking of something you are afraid of; and Situational (Si), which occur while you are in the feared situation.*

Date	Average Anxiety	Average Depression	Average Worry about Panic

Your Daily Mood Record for Overcoming Panic Attacks*

It is important to keep track of your moods to overcome your panic attacks. At the end of each day, put a rating in each column using a ten-point scale, where 0 = *none* and 10 = *extreme*.

How to do Deep Breathing to Manage Your Anxiety*

Deep breathing is a simple technique that can be used to help with stress relief, anxiety management, mood improvement, and general well-being. It works best if you practice for about ten minutes a day on a consistent basis. Find a place and time where you will not be disturbed. Let people in your home know that this is a time when you need to be alone.
To get started, you may find it easier to lie down on the floor. Use pillows under your head and knees for comfort.

- Place one hand on your lower abdomen.
- Breathe in deeply and slowly as you count to five, pulling your breath into your lower abdomen until it raises the hand that is resting there.
- Release your breath slowly and smoothly as you count to five.
- Focus on your breath as you do this exercise.

Once you have mastered the technique, you can do this without using your hand on your abdomen.

If you prefer not to lie on the floor, you can practice sitting up in a chair. Use your hand on your lower abdomen until you get used to bringing your breath down deep.

Try to relax your body and your mind as you breathe. If you are distracted, simply bring your attention back to your breath. You may enjoy playing some soft, relaxing music or nature sounds.

VIDEO DEMONSTRATION: This video from the Harvard School of Public Health shows Dr. Lillian Cheung demonstrating mindful breathing. Join the class! It runs just over 13 minutes. Link: http://youtu.be/8c-1Ylieg3g.

Once you get into the habit of deep breathing, you will find it easier to use this technique to calm yourself down when you start having thoughts that would normally make you feel anxious and might bring on a panic attack.

Calming Your Body with Progressive Muscle Relaxation*

Progressive muscle relaxation is a technique that involves tensing specific muscle groups and then relaxing them. It is termed "progressive" because you relax all major muscle groups—starting at the head and working your way down to your feet, relaxing them one at a time. In only 10 to 15 minutes you can achieve total body relaxation.

Progressive Muscle Relaxation is a particularly effective relaxation technique because it enables you to focus on your body tension. There are many other relaxation techniques that can help you reduce your anxiety, but this technique may be most helpful for people who have body complaints that often accompany high levels of stress and anxiety, such as headaches, stomach problems, or muscle pain. When you are ready to try this technique, find a place where you won't be disturbed or distracted for at least 15 minutes. Recline in a comfortable chair or on a mat and take a few deep breaths to begin the exercise. Use the following audio to help you learn this technique. This audio was recorded at the McKinley Health Center at the University of Illinois and will guide you through your progressive relaxation. Enter the link in your browser, and you can play the audio right from your computer. Time: 12 minutes.

https://www.betweensessions.com/wp-content/uploads/2017/03/progressive_muscle_relaxation_audio.mp3

You can also download the audio to your computer as an mp3 file by right-clicking on the screen and selecting "save as." You can then attach your smartphone or music player to your computer and copy it to a playlist. After listening for a few times, you can practice this relaxation technique without the audio if you wish, but remember to relax for at least 10 minutes.

Relaxation techniques can be very effective in reducing anxiety, but only when you practice these techniques regularly. When you practice relaxation techniques for at least 10 minutes a day, you will train your brain and body to "calm down" on demand. As soon as you start to feel anxious, you can take a few deep breaths and think about how it feels to be calm, which automatically sends a message to your brain, telling it to "calm down," and to your body to release your muscle tension.

Taking 10 minutes a day to practice relaxation techniques will not only help you control your anxiety but may also have other health benefits. There are many different kinds of relaxation techniques and they all appear to have the same healthful effect on the mind and body. Some research suggests that relaxation techniques can aid the body in the healing process and help in controlling high blood pressure, coping with chronic pain, controlling asthma, and aiding with sleep problems. Many medical professionals believe that daily relaxation exercises will aid in preventing disease, reducing elevated levels of cortisol (the stress hormone), and bolstering the immune system. Use the chart on the next page to help you create a habit of relaxing every day.

Keeping Track of Your Relaxation Practice

Use the chart below to record your daily relaxation "habit." Make copies of this chart and keep recording the time you spend relaxing until it is truly a habit—something you do without thinking, like brushing your teeth.

Today's date: _____

	Time of Day	Minutes	Mood Before	Mood After
Sunday				
Monday				
Tuesday				
Wednesday				
Thursday				
Friday				
Saturday				

The Grounding Technique*

Grounding Techniques are a set of tools used to assist individuals to stay in the present moment during episodes of intense anxiety or other overwhelming emotions. Staying in the present moment allows people to feel safe and in control by focusing on the physical world and how they experience it.

Grounding is easy to do. Just focus on some aspect of the physical world, rather than on your internal thoughts and feelings (see suggestions below). Focus on the present rather than the past. Practice your grounding techniques so that they will come naturally when you are upset. Let go of any negative feelings. Try a variety of techniques and, on the next page, rate the effectiveness of each technique in keeping you calm. Have others assist you in using these techniques by reminding you to practice them and use them as soon as you are feeling emotionally distressed.

You can view a video of how a therapist helps a client with PTSD using the Grounding Technique from the National Center for Post Traumatic Stress Disorder by going to: (https://youtu.be/DFxRs1oFiEE)

Here are some Grounding Technique suggestions, but you can make up your own as well.

- Run cool water over your hands.

- Grab tightly onto your chair as hard as you can.

- Touch various objects around you: a pen, keys, your clothing, or the wall.

- Dig your heels into the floor, literally "grounding" them! Notice the tension centered in your heels as you do this. Remind yourself you are connected to the ground.

- Carry a grounding object in your pocket, which you can touch whenever you feel triggered.

- Notice your body: the weight of your body in the chair; wiggle your toes in your socks; notice the feel of your chair against your back …

- Stretch. Roll your head around.

- Clench and release your fists.

- Walk slowly; notice each footstep, saying "left or "right"… to yourself.

- Focus on your breathing … notice each inhale and exhale.

- Eat something, describing the flavors to yourself.

Other ideas: _____

_____

_____

_____

_____

_____

_____

_____

_____

_____

_____

_____

_____

_____

_____

_____

_____

_____

_____

_____

_____

_____

_____

_____

Recording Your Use of the Grounding Technique

Begin by writing in five or more techniques you want to practice. Practice them several times a day for five minutes or until you feel calm and in control.

Circle the number that best describes the effectiveness of each technique.

1 = no effect, 2 = little effect, 3 = effective but took time,

4 = effective in keeping me calm and focused, 5 = immediate calming effect

Technique	Date Started	Rating					Comments
		1	2	3	4	5	
		1	2	3	4	5	
		1	2	3	4	5	
		1	2	3	4	5	
		1	2	3	4	5	
		1	2	3	4	5	
		1	2	3	4	5	
		1	2	3	4	5	
		1	2	3	4	5	
		1	2	3	4	5	
		1	2	3	4	5	
		1	2	3	4	5	
		1	2	3	4	5	
		1	2	3	4	5	

Becoming Aware of Your Upsetting Thoughts and Feelings

Many people deal with their problems by trying to avoid painful thoughts, feelings, sensations, and memories. They think that if they just distract themselves from these inner experiences, then they will be fine.

However, while avoiding these unpleasant inner experiences may help temporarily, these strategies usually only work for a short period of time. There is also a significant personal cost to your avoidance. Some people spend hours each day avoiding the things that could upset them instead of using this time to enjoy life. This worksheet is designed to help you examine how you are avoiding the things that cause you to be anxious and upset, and how this keeps you from having a happier and more fulfilling life.

Begin by listing the inner experiences you are trying to avoid.

List three <u>thoughts</u> that upset you.

_____

_____

_____

List three <u>feelings</u> that upset you.

_____

_____

_____

List three <u>sensations</u> that upset you.

_____

_____

_____

List three <u>memories</u> that upset you.

_____

_____

_____

Write any additional upsetting thoughts, feelings, sensations, or memories here.

_____

_____

_____

Now think about the things you do to avoid these unpleasant inner experiences.

List the things you do to <u>distract</u> yourself from unpleasant inner experiences.

_____

_____

_____

List the <u>activities</u> or <u>events</u> you avoid to keep from having painful inner experiences.

_____

_____

_____

List the <u>places</u> you avoid to keep from having painful inner experiences.

_____

_____

_____

List the <u>people</u> you avoid to keep from having painful inner experiences.

_____

_____

_____

List substances—including alcohol, cigarettes, drugs, and food—you use to try and avoid unpleasant inner experiences.

_____

_____

_____

Is there anything else you do to avoid unpleasant or painful inner experiences?

_____

_____

_____

Now go back to what you have written and circle the three things you do most often to avoid unpleasant inner experiences.

In the space below, write down how your life might be different if you could accept these unpleasant inner experiences rather than work so hard to avoid them.

_____

_____

_____

_____

_____

_____

_____

_____

_____

_____

_____

_____

_____

_____

Tolerating Your Distressing Thoughts & Feelings with Mindfulness

When you are prone to anxiety or panic attacks, just thinking about something can make you upset and cause your body to react. Your thoughts can trigger a fear response in your body, like a tightness in your chest or shallow breathing. Sometimes, this can result in a full-blown panic attack, and you can even feel like you are having a heart-attack. All this can start with just a simple thought.

This mindfulness exercise is designed to help you be aware of upsetting thoughts, without letting them trigger a physical anxiety response in your body.

Being mindful means acknowledging your thoughts and feelings without responding to them in a typically negative way. Mindfulness is a technique that increases your awareness of the present moment while being non-judgmental. Being non-judgmental is the key, and that's what we're going to work on with this exercise.

Begin by sitting in a comfortable chair. Now read the unpleasant phrases below and pick one to visualize. Take your time (at least five minutes) visualizing the image and use all the appropriate senses. Experience the sounds and the smells you associate with this image and the taste and touch if appropriate.

Even though the images these phrases provoke may be repellant, don't judge them. See if you can be aware of them without any negative reaction.

1. A person vomiting on you

2. Opening a door and finding a dead animal in the room

3. Looking at an open, oozing sore

4. Sitting in a dark cave with insects crawling around you

Can you think of other images which would be repellant to you?

5. _____

6. _____

7. _____

Practice this mindful technique with two more phrases for five minutes each. Rate how you did with each image, using the scale: 1 = "I didn't respond to the image at all" and 7 = "I was completely disgusted by the image."

Now, write down one situation that normally causes you to be very anxious and upset:

_____

Practice this same exercise, thinking about this situation in a mindful and non-judgmental manner at least once a day for at least seven days. Use this page to record your progress.

Situation That Causes You to Be Anxious	Date and Time of Practice	Rating

Tolerating the Physical Discomfort from Your Anxiety

It's common for people to experience physical discomfort when they are fearful and anxious. If you start thinking about a speech you have to deliver or being in an enclosed place, or going to a crowded concert, your heart might start beating faster, your chest may tighten, you may sweat and even feel like you are going to faint.

These physical reactions can be very scary, and some people say they feel like they are having a heart attack or that they feel removed from reality. When this happens, people can become just as afraid of the physical reaction as they are of the actual situation that causes their anxiety. This is what some call "the fear of fear."

However, there is one proven way to break this cycle of anxiety and fear: to practice the physical sensations that make you nervous and panicky. If this doesn't sound like fun, you're right, it isn't. However, there are many studies that tell us that this is an important step to take in conquering your anxiety.

There are three parts to this exercise. The first part is to determine the physical sensations that accompany your anxiety. You do this in the first column of the chart on the next page. Circle the physical symptoms you are most likely to have when you are feeling anxious and panicky.

The second part of this exercise is to actually create these uncomfortable feelings. The second column on the chart on the next page will give you some ideas how to do this. *Note*: You should initially practice these several times with a coach or friend in the room. The coach will encourage you to perform the exercises so that you mimic the physical sensations associated with your anxiety and will also protect you from any possible physical injury, like falling if you get dizzy.

The third and final part of this exercise is to record your practice recreating the physical discomfort that you associate with your fear and anxiety. Although this isn't pleasant, the more you practice, the sooner you will be able to master your anxiety and lead a more energetic and fulfilling life.

Recreating Your Physical Discomfort

The more you practice the physical feelings that you associate with anxiety and panic, the less likely you are to be influenced by these feelings. To prevent any possible injury, you should practice these physical exercises in the presence of a supportive person and in an appropriate place.

Uncomfortable Feelings	Creating Those Feelings
Lightheadedness, feeling faint	• Hyperventilate for one minute. Breathe loudly and rapidly (similar to a panting dog) at a rate of approximately 45 breaths per minute. • Place your head between your legs for one minute, then quickly sit up.
Feeling weird and unreal	• Think of how big the universe is and how small you are. • Think about the 200,000 years that humans have been on the earth as well as all of your ancestors. • Sit in a completely dark and completely quiet room for five minutes.
Blurred vision	• Stare at a lightbulb for one minute and then attempt to read.
Difficulty breathing	• Hold your nose and breathe through a thin straw for one minute.
Increased heart rate or tightness in your chest	• Drink an espresso or other caffeine-based drink. • Do five minutes of moderately intensive cardiovascular exercise like running up and down the stairs
Upset stomach	• Do 20 jumping jacks after a meal.
Feeling shaky	• Tense all of your muscles and hold the tension for one minute.
Sweating	• Wear a jacket or wrap yourself in a blanket in a hot room.
Feeling dizzy	• Spin around really fast for one minute.
Write other physical problems you have when you are anxious	How can you replicate these feelings?

Practicing Being Physically Uncomfortable

The phrase "practice makes perfect" has never been truer than for people overcoming feelings of anxiety and panic. Although it is not pleasant, practicing the uncomfortable feelings that accompany your anxiety will help you control your emotions rather than having them control you. Use this chart to record the time and dates of your practice as well as your reactions. Rate your anxiety about each session from 1 = no anxiety to 10 = a great deal of anxiety.

Date and Time	Physical Feeling	Rating

Stop Avoiding Situations that Make You Anxious

Many people deal with their anxiety and panic attacks by simply avoiding the situations that cause them to be fearful. While avoidance may reduce anxiety in the short term, it will also restrict your life unnecessarily and possibly exacerbate your fears and worries in the long run. To conquer your fears and anxiety, you must learn to tolerate the situations that bother you, rather than avoid them. I know this sounds difficult, but study after study tells us that this is the best way to rid yourself of anxiety. The first step is to prioritize the situations that you avoid because they make you anxious.

Put a number by the situations or places you avoid when you are alone because they make you anxious. Put a number 1 by the situation/place you avoid most, a number two by the situation you avoid, next and so on.

_____ Airplanes

_____ Subways

_____ Buses or trains

_____ Boats or ships

_____ Theaters

_____ Shopping centers

_____ Supermarkets

_____ Standing in lines

_____ Auditoriums or stadiums

_____ Parties or other social gatherings

_____ Crowds

_____ Restaurants

_____ Museums

_____ Elevators

_____ Enclosed spaces

_____ Tunnels

_____ Driving or riding in a car

_____ Large rooms, such as the lobby in a hotel

_____ Walking on the street

_____ Courtyards

_____ High places

_____ Traveling away from home

_____ Staying home alone

_____ Crossing bridges

_____ Other _____

_____ Other _____

_____ Other _____

_____ Other _____

What Are the Odds?

Many people avoid certain situations because of their fears and worries. Although they are otherwise rational people, they view certain situations with "catastrophic thinking," meaning that they treat a common situation as if a catastrophe were going to occur, even though the odds of this happening are extremely low. Take a look at these examples of people who avoid common situations because of their catastrophic thinking:

> Although Jonathon traveled every week for his job, he had a terrible fear of bridges and avoided them at all cost. He kept imagining that the bridge he was on would fall down and he would plummet to his death. He was terrified every time he had to drive over a bridge. *Jonathon had this fear, even though he had never heard of a bridge just falling down. In fact, he looked it up and found that there are 6 million bridges in the US and there have only been 111 collapses in 150 years.*

> Sarah had a weekly meeting with her manager, who was very intimidating. On the night before her meeting, Sarah worried that she would tremble and sweat during her meeting or even pass out, even though everyone in the office thought of her as very calm and in control. *In fact, Sarah had never shown any of the physical signs of being anxious at the office or anywhere else.*

> Tanya avoided going to the cinema and always made excuses when her eight-year-old asked to be taken to the latest animated film. Tanya didn't like to feel "closed in" and felt that she might scream or do something crazy in front of her son. *She believed this even though she had never lost her cool before.*

Catastrophic thinking is a type of irrational thinking that is very common in people with anxiety disorders and particularly people who have panic attacks. This type of thinking makes people avoid situations out of fear, and avoiding the situations tends to reinforce this type of thinking. However, it is important to remember that the more you avoid the situations that make you fearful, the more power you give them. The best way to conquer your feelings of anxiety and panic are to face the situations you are currently avoiding. This worksheet is designed to help you think rationally about the situations you are avoiding and to see that the odds of something bad happening are extremely remote.

Write down the one situation you try hardest to avoid because you are afraid something terrible will happen.

_____

What are you afraid will happen?

_____

_____

Has the situation that makes you anxious ever happened to you before?

_____

What is the likelihood (odds) this will happen?

_____

What are the reasons this probably won't happen?

_____

_____

_____

What is the very worst thing that could *likely* happen?

_____

_____

List some things you think about that cause you to worry, even though you know these things aren't true.

_____

_____

What magical rituals do you do when you can't avoid a feared situation?

_____

_____

What will happen if you stop doing these?

_____

_____

What positive thing might help you face your fears? For example, getting support from someone you trust to help you confront the situation you have been avoiding.

_____

_____

_____

_____

Talking Back to the Thoughts that Make You Anxious

Cognitive Behavioral Therapy (CBT) is designed to help you change the irrational thoughts that fuel your anxiety and panic attacks. Your irrational thoughts (also called cognitive distortions) are based on errors in thinking rather than on fact. When you learn to talk back to your irrational thoughts with fact-based logic, then you will diminish your anxiety and it will be easier to face your fears.

This worksheet lists 18 irrational thoughts commonly held by people who experience anxiety and panic attacks. Each statement is followed by a "talk-back" statement which is reality based.

Begin this exercise by reading all of these statements carefully, paying particular attention to the "talk-back" arguments. Focus on the logic in each "talk-back" statement and why these statements are true.

Then on the next page, go over the irrational statements again and write in a rational "talk-back" statement. It doesn't have to be exactly the same, it just has to be logical and based on fact.

Finally, think of any other irrational thoughts that fuel your anxiety and panic attacks. Write them down and then write down the rational fact-based "talk-back" statement.

Step 1: Begin by reading the common thoughts that occur to people with panic attacks, thinking about the rational "talk-back" statements and how they are grounded in fact rather than fear.

1. My panic attack will cause me to have a heart attack.
   Talk-back: Panic attacks can simulate symptoms of a heart attack, but these symptoms are not dangerous and soon pass. I don't have to be afraid of them.

2. If I'm in a crowd, I will faint.
   Talk-back: If I feel light headed or dizzy, I can just breathe deeply and slowly to get more oxygen. I've never fainted in a crowd before.

3. I'm going crazy.
   Talk-back: Anxiety can play tricks on my mind, but these thoughts and feelings will soon pass. Being afraid does not mean I'm going crazy.

4. People will think I'm weird because I'm so anxious about everything.
   Talk-back: Lots of people have problems with anxiety. Everyone knows what it feels like to be anxious.

5. People will think less of me because I'm so anxious.
Talk-back: Most people do not judge others harshly. If someone doesn't like something about me, that really doesn't affect me.

6. I will do something inappropriate in a crowded situation (or other feared situation), and people will think I'm crazy or I could even get into trouble.
Talk-back: The fear of doing something inappropriate in public is just a thought I'm having now. I have never done anything like this before.

7. Something terrible will happen if I _____ (fill in a situation that you are avoiding).

Talk-back: This is an example of catastrophic thinking. It's a symptom of my panic attacks and is not reality based. The probability of this happening is almost non-existent.

8. I must do well and win the approval of others, or else I am no good.
Talk-back: My self-worth is not based on what others think of me. I don't have to be perfect. Everyone makes mistakes some of the time.

9. I need people to see me as strong and competent.

Talk-back: My feelings of self-worth come from inside me, not from others. Self-worth primarily comes from my actions, and I can do _____ to increase my positive feelings.

10. If people find out at work that I have anxiety attacks, I won't get good evaluations or promotions.

Talk-back: Success at work is almost always based on work performance. If my anxiety ever interferes with my work performance, I can get feedback and help to stop this from happening.

11. If I have a panic attack and I must leave the room, people will think I'm crazy.
Talk-back: I don't have to leave the room when I feel panicky. I know these feelings will soon pass and I can just let them go.

12. I can't let anyone find out I have panic attacks; I must keep them a secret.

Talk-back: Many people suffer from problems with anxiety, including panic attacks. Hiding my problem doesn't help. Facing my fears is the only way to get rid of them for good.

13. If I had a panic attack while at _____, I would be so embarrassed I would never be able to face anyone again.

    Talk-back: The nature of my panic attacks is that I fear things that are not true. Even if in the unlikely event I had a panic attack in public, most people would not notice, and if anyone did notice, I would explain what happened later. There is no shame in having a problem with anxiety.

14. I must always have other people's approval, or else I feel worthless.

    Talk-back: My self-confidence and self-worth do not depend on what other people think of me. Everyone has self-doubt at some time, but I know what to do regain my confidence.

15. If someone rejects me, I am a failure.

    Talk-back: Rejection is a part of life. No one can succeed all of the time. I'm not going to base my actions on a fear of rejection.

16. I must be perceived as a strong person, and panic attacks make me look weak.

    Talk-back: I can't control the way that people judge me.

17. I will always have panic attacks.

    Talk-back: I can develop the skills to face my fears and get rid of panic attacks forever.

18. I can't travel because of my anxiety and panic attacks.

    Talk-back: I am not going to give into my fears and restrict my life.

Step 2: Now write down your own "talk-back" statements arguing with these common irrational thoughts. You don't have to remember exactly what was said in the examples, just use your own words and make sure your thoughts are based on reality.

1. My panic attack will cause me to have a heart attack.
   Talk-back:

   _____

   _____

   _____

2. If I'm in a crowd, I will faint.
   Talk-back:

   _____

   _____

   _____

3. I'm going crazy.
   Talk-back:

   _____

   _____

   _____

4. People will think I'm weird because I'm so anxious about everything.
   Talk-back:

   _____

   _____

   _____

5. People will think less of me because I'm so anxious.
   Talk-back:

   _____

   _____

   _____

6. I will do something inappropriate in a crowded situation (or other feared situation) and people will think I'm crazy, or I could even get into trouble.
   Talk-back:

   _____

   _____

   _____

7. Something terrible will happen if I _____ (fill in a situation that you are avoiding).
   Talk-back:

   _____

   _____

   _____

8. I must do well and win the approval of others, or else I am no good.
   Talk-back:

   _____

   _____

   _____

9. I need people to see me as strong and competent.
   Talk-back:

   _____

   _____

   _____

10. If people find out at work that I have anxiety attacks, I won't get good evaluations or promotions.
    Talk-back:

    _____

    _____

    _____

11. If I have a panic attack and I must leave the room, people will think I'm crazy.
    Talk-back:

    _____

    _____

    _____

12. I can't let anyone find out I have panic attacks; I must keep them a secret.
Talk-back:

_____

_____

13. If I had a panic attack while at _____, I would be so embarrassed I would never be able to face anyone again.
Talk-back:

_____

_____

_____

14. I must always have other people's approval, or else I feel worthless.
Talk-back:

_____

_____

_____

15. If someone rejects me, I am a failure.
Talk-back:

_____

_____

_____

16. I must be perceived as a strong person, and panic attacks make me look weak.
Talk-back:

_____

_____

_____

17. I will always have panic attacks.
    Talk-back:

    _____

    _____

    _____

18. I can't travel because of my anxiety and panic attacks.
    Talk-back:

    _____

    _____

    _____

Step 3: Now write down other thoughts that make you anxious and how you would talk back to them using fact-based logic.

Irrational fear-based thought:

_____

_____

Talk-back:

_____

_____

Irrational fear-based thought:

_____

_____

Talk-back:

_____

_____

Irrational fear-based thought:

_____

_____

Talk-back:

_____

Irrational fear-based thought:

_____

_____

Talk-back:

_____

_____

Irrational fear-based thought:

_____

_____

Talk-back:

_____

_____

Irrational fear-based thought:

_____

_____

Talk-back:

_____

_____

Using Coping Statements to Deal with Your Panic Attacks

Accepting your thoughts and feelings can help you move past your fears and anxiety and create a new way of looking at your life. Read through the statements below and put a check by the statements that sound like you. Then, write down the statements you have checked on a separate piece of paper and read them to yourself when you feel that your emotions are getting out of control. Take a few deep breaths before you begin, relax your body, and try to adopt a non-judgmental attitude.

_____ I can't change what has already happened.

_____ I'm not going to drive myself crazy with things I can't change.

_____ Dwelling on the past keeps me from appreciating what is in the present.

_____ I can accept things the way they are.

_____ This feels bad, but it is a normal reaction and will pass.

_____ I have dealt with problems before and I can deal with this.

_____ Thoughts are just happening in my brain, they are not THE TRUTH.

_____ I can learn from the past to solve present and future problems.

_____ I can get through this.

_____ This is difficult but it is temporary.

_____ If I stop and calm myself down, then I can get through this.

_____ These are just feelings and will go away.

_____ I can feel badly, but still act in ways that are good for me and good for others.

_____ I don't need to change everything at once.

_____ I can accept myself the way I am.

_____ I can accept my situation for what it is and still be happy.

_____ It's okay to feel this way.

Write down other statements that can help you cope.

_____

_____

_____

Examining Your Success at Using Coping Statements

After rehearsing the coping statements that you find most meaningful, you can use this worksheet to determine whether they are effective in dealing with your fears and anxiety.

Write down distressing thoughts and feelings you are having.

_____

_____

_____

_____

_____

Write down the coping statement that you used.

_____

_____

_____

_____

_____

Rate how anxious and fearful you felt <u>before</u> reading the coping statement _____

        1 = not very upset   10 = as upset and distressed as I get

Rate how anxious and fearful you felt <u>after</u> reading the coping statement _____

        1 = not very upset   10 = as upset and distressed as I get

Write down how your behavior changed as a result of using positive coping statements.

_____

_____

_____

_____

Controlling Your Anxiety with a "Worry Script"

Many people spend hours each day trying to avoid worrying about things that upset them. People distract themselves by watching TV, focusing on a new worry to avoid thinking about an old one, or even self-medicating with drinking, drugs, or overeating. None of these things help reduce worrying.

In fact, most people find that the harder they try to avoid the thoughts that make them anxious, the worse they get. Trying to push something out of your mind is a little like trying to push a beach ball underwater: it takes a lot of work to keep it down, and the minute you let it go, it pops right back up again.

Rather than putting all your energy into avoiding upsetting thoughts and images, you can choose to face your fears, and writing worry scripts is one way to help you do this. By writing a worry script about your biggest worry, you will be facing your negative thoughts and upsetting feelings rather than trying to avoid them. Writing scripts will also help you get a clear picture of what is really upsetting you. Many people who write a worry script for a few weeks report that they feel less anxious about the things they were worrying about.

How to write a worry script:
- Choose a place where you won't be interrupted. Turn off your cell phone, music, and television. Set aside about 30 minutes to complete each script.
- Write about one thing you are worrying about.
- Write about the worst-case scenario of one of your worries. For example, if you are worrying about your child getting bullied in school, write about the worst events that could happen to your child and the worst ways he or she might react.
- Write a script that is vivid and includes how things look, sound, and feel. Include your feelings and reactions.
- Write a new script on the same subject each day, going deeper into your feelings with each script.
- After about two weeks, you can move to the next worry.

NOTE: If you feel anxious and even tearful while you are writing, keep at it! Experiencing these feelings means you are on the right track. Even though it may be difficult, the more you face your fears and worries, the more likely they will eventually fade.

My Worry Script

Date: _____ Beginning Time: _____ Ending Time: _____

Summarize what you are worrying about in a sentence:

_____

Describe your worry in vivid detail:

_____

_____

_____

_____

_____

_____

_____

_____

_____

_____

_____

_____

_____

_____

_____

Practicing Getting Anxious

It is perfectly understandable to avoid the things that make you anxious, but this is actually the worst thing you can do. We all experience reasonable anxiety sometimes, like when you are driving at night in a storm. But we're talking about recurring problems with anxiety and fear that are not based in reality. This would include situations like going over a bridge, being in a crowded elevator, the fear of public speaking, and so on. In these situations, your brain may trick you into feeling that something terrible will happen, but in fact, these situations are only mildly unpleasant, like many things you experience throughout the day. There is no reason to avoid them, and doing so may significantly constrict your life.

The key to overcoming your anxiety is to learn to tolerate the situations that make you worried and fearful, and this takes practice. This worksheet is designed to help you "practice getting anxious." This may not be easy. But the more you practice, the sooner you will be able to overcome your problems with anxiety and fear.

Practice Worksheet

Today's date: _____

Step 1: Choose to get anxious.

Write down the one thing you will intentionally do today that will make you anxious. List the time of day you will practice getting anxious.

_____

Time _____

Step 2: Stay with your symptoms by just observing and accepting them.

Instead of trying to run away from your anxiety and the physical symptoms that accompany your feelings, just let your reactions happen and dispassionately observe them. For example, if you feel your heart start to beat faster, say to yourself, "I'm upset and I can feel my heart racing, but I know that it is just my mind playing tricks on me. There is nothing to be afraid of. It will pass."

Write down something you can say to yourself that will help you tolerate your symptoms.

_____

_____

_____

Step 3: Let go of your safety crutches.

Write down three things you might normally do to avoid your anxiety, such as telling yourself you aren't feeling well enough to face your fears, using some magical ritual, or insisting on having a friend stay with you for support. These are your safety crutches. Make sure you don't use them when you practice facing your anxiety.

_____

_____

_____

Step 4: Stop yourself from overreacting.

Many people with anxiety problems immediately think of the very worst thing that could happen to them if they face their fears. For example, a person afraid to ride in an elevator might worry that the elevator will break down between floors or that the elevator cable will snap. This is called "catastrophic thinking," which means that you only think about the very worst thing that could happen even though the probability of this happening is extremely small.

In the space below, write down the worst thing you think could happen if you face the things that cause your anxiety and fears. Then write down why these thoughts are unreasonable.

The very worst thing that could happen is:

_____

_____

_____

The reasons that this is almost impossible are:

_____

_____

_____

Step 5: Decide how long you can tolerate your anxious symptoms.

Minutes planned_____

Minutes actual _____

Step 6: Rate how successful you were in tolerating your anxiety, where 1 = not successful at all, and 10 = very successful.

Rating: _____

Write down any thoughts or feelings you had about this practice session.

_____

_____

_____

_____

_____

_____

_____

_____

_____

_____

_____

_____

_____

_____

Eliminating Unhelpful Coping Strategies

Panic attacks are very scary, so it is only natural to try and avoid them at all costs. But studies tell us that avoiding your panic attacks and the other things that make you anxious is the worst thing you can do. In fact, most of the things that people do to protect themselves from panic attacks are unhelpful and just prolong this problem. This worksheet is designed to help you identify the things you do to "protect" yourself from panic attacks. Remember, there is no need for protection from danger that doesn't exist. Giving up these unhelpful strategies will help you rid yourself of panic attacks forever.

List the situations you avoid because you are afraid they may trigger a panic attack. Then rate each one on how hard it will be to give this up, where 1 = not hard at all, and 10 = extremely hard.

List any rituals you use in the hope that they will magically keep panic attacks from occurring.

_____ Rating _____

_____ Rating _____

_____ Rating _____

_____ Rating _____

List any ways you distract yourself when you are anxious about having a panic attack.

_____ Rating _____

_____ Rating _____

_____ Rating _____

List any people you feel you *must* have with you in situations you think might trigger a panic attack.

_____ Rating _____

_____ Rating _____

_____ Rating _____

List any objects that you feel magically protect you from having a panic attack.

_____ Rating _____

_____ Rating _____

_____ Rating _____

Are there things you must "check" several times when you feel anxious?

_____ Rating _____

_____ Rating _____

_____ Rating _____

List the unhelpful strategies you are ready to give up, starting with the ones with the lowest rating:

_____

_____

_____

_____

_____

_____

_____

_____

_____

Creating an Exposure Hierarchy to Overcome Your Fears

Decades of research tells us that the best way to overcome your fears is to face them in small sequential steps. To do this, you can create an Exposure Hierarchy, which will gradually "expose" you to the situations that you fear until you can face your fears with a minimum of concern. Avoiding your fears never helps and, in fact, may even make them worse.

This technique works with different kinds of fears and specific situations that make you anxious or trigger a panic attack. In many ways, it is the most important part of treating your panic attacks because it will allow you to do things you may have been avoiding for years.

The goals of exposure therapy include:

- doing things you have been avoiding
- reducing anxiety and fear of a panic attack
- enjoying activities again
- feeling more control in your life

Measuring Your Distress

Anxiety is commonly measured by a scale called the Subjective Units of Distress Scale or SUDS. This scale goes from zero to 100. Zero means you have no distress, 50 means you have moderate distress, while 100 means you have the worst distress you can imagine.

Creating Your Exposure Hierarchy

1. To begin, pick one fear you would like to work on. This could be a fear of crowds, a fear of enclosed places, or a fear of flying. Write down the fear that is most likely to cause a panic attack.

2. On the next page (Situations that Trigger Your Fear), write down specific situations that cause you to be fearful and anxious, rating each with a SUDS score. It will be easiest to work on your problem if you list at least 10 to 15 situations related to your fear. For example, if you are afraid of flying you might list: thinking about a trip, going to the airport, waiting for the flight, take-off, turbulence, and so on.

3. Then, on the worksheet "Prioritizing the Situations that Trigger Your Fear," you should reorder the fears you have written down, starting with the fear that has the lowest SUDS score.

4. Finally, you will "expose" yourself to each situation and record your response using the worksheet "Practicing Exposure Therapy." This simply means that you will try to

recreate each situation that causes you to be fearful. If possible, you will literally reenact the situation that causes your fear, starting with the situation that causes the least anxiety (i.e., lowest SUDS score) and working your way up. For example, if you were afraid of being in a crowded elevator in a skyscraper, you would start by going in an elevator just one floor by yourself. Then you might go to the second floor, and so on. When you could ride the elevator to the top floor by yourself, you would gradually ride the elevator at a time of day when it would likely be more crowded. Finally, you will be able to ride a crowded elevator to the very top floor.

With some fears, you will not be able to actually reenact each situation in your exposure hierarchy. Going back to the example of overcoming a fear of flying, you will not be able to actually practice something like a fear of turbulence since this is obviously unpredictable. When you can't reenact the actual experience, you can first practice by imagining how this might feel. This is called imaginal exposure, and can be surprisingly effective. You can also approximate the physical feeling you are learning to tolerate. For example, to experience the physical sensation of turbulence, you might shut your eyes and sway your body in different directions.

You should note that facing your fear does not mean you will be completely calm and carefree. On the contrary, you will likely still feel some anxiety and distress but in the lower range of the SUDS scale. Tolerating some anxiety and distress is simply part of life.

Situations That Trigger Your Fear and Anxiety

Enter a fear you would like to address on the line provided. Enter specific situations you avoid related to that fear. Enter one situation per line. Try to list as many as you can. Next, rate each situation according to how much anxiety the situation triggers, from 0 = no anxiety to 100 = the most anxiety you can imagine.

The fear I am working on is: _____

Today's date: _____

	Situations that Trigger Your Fear and Anxiety	SUDS Score
1		
2		
3		
4		
5		
6		
7		
8		
9		
10		
11		
12		
13		
14		
15		

Prioritizing the Situations that Trigger Your Fear/Anxiety

Reorder the situations that cause your fear/anxiety from the lowest SUDS score to the highest.

Fear you are working on: _____

Today's date: _____

	Situation that Triggers this Fear	SUDS Score
1		
2		
3		
4		
5		
6		
7		
8		
9		
10		
11		
12		
13		
14		
15		

Practicing Exposure Therapy

Write down what you are doing to face your fear and anxiety.

_____

_____

Record each exposure session, noting your SUDS rating *before*, *during*, and *after* each session.

	Date/Time/Place	SUDS Rating (0-100)		
		Pre	Peak	Post
1				
2				
3				
4				
5				
6				
7				
8				
9				
10				
11				
12				

Overcoming Setbacks in Overcoming Your Panic Attacks

Overcoming your panic attacks take a lot of work, and you may experience setbacks for a variety of reasons.

For example, Jonathon used to get panic attacks thinking about making a presentation to his class. Sometimes he would drop a class because a presentation was coming up and he started having panic attacks. With work and lots of practice, Johnathon was able to make presentations without worrying about panic attacks.

But at the end of his senior year, Jonathon had to do a 30-minute presentation in his philosophy class. The week before the presentation, when he was lying in bed thinking about how he would organize it, his heart started to race. The more he tried to ignore it, the worse he felt, and soon he recognized that he was starting to have a full-fledged panic attack.

Setbacks can occur for many reasons. They most commonly occur when you stop practicing your skills for overcoming panic and facing the things you were avoiding. They can also occur when you are under a lot of stress. Other times a setback can occur because they are triggered by a certain event. Sometimes a setback can occur because of a change in your lifestyle (sleeping, eating, exercise) or because you have made some unhealthy choices like drinking too much or taking drugs.

Don't be upset if you have a setback in dealing with your anxiety. Setbacks are common because stress and change in your life are constant. And don't let setbacks give you the feeling that you are back to where you started. Setbacks are temporary, just a sign that you need to pay attention to the kind of life you want to live every day.

The easiest way to avoid setbacks is to prepare for them. Filling out this worksheet will help you think about the kinds of things that can cause a setback and recognize the early signs that your panic attacks may be recurring. Answer these questions thoroughly and honestly.

Write down the most likely situations that could cause a setback.

_____

_____

What are some specific triggers—including people, places, thoughts, and behaviors—that might cause a setback?

_____

_____

What are some early signs that might mean you are having a setback?

_____

_____

Write down two or three people you can ask to tell you if they see early signs of a setback.

_____

_____

Have you started doing anything to avoid situations that caused your original panic attacks?

_____

_____

Have you started doing anything to mask your anxiety (e.g., drinking, taking drugs, or other escapist behavior)?

_____

_____

Have you had any changes in medication that might be affecting your mood?

_____

_____

Are you having negative thoughts about yourself that you know are not really true? What are they?

_____

_____

What are the most effective skills you learned to deal with your original problem?

_____

_____

What is the most important skill you can use if you see an early sign of having panic attacks?

_____

_____

Makes a list of at least five things you can do avoid having a setback:

_____

_____

_____

_____

_____

_____

_____

_____

_____

_____

_____

_____

_____

_____

_____

Getting More Sleep Can Help Reduce Your Anxiety

Do you have a hard time falling to sleep or staying asleep? A lack of sleep will reduce the serotonin levels in your brain, which may make it harder to control your moods during the day. There are a variety of techniques that can help you get the sleep you need, but, of course, they only work if you are diligent at trying them and then using the ones that work best. Getting enough sleep is an important part of your overall plan to overcome your anxiety and is also important for your general health.

There are a variety of medications available to help you sleep, including prescription medication, herbs, and supplements, but always consult a physician before taking any kind of sleep aid.

Here are some other things you can try. Keep track of your sleep and the methods you use to sleep better on the chart on the next page. Track your progress for at least two weeks.

Techniques to Help You Get More Sleep

- Listen to soft music, read, take a warm shower, or meditate before going to bed.
- Exercise for at least a half-hour each day, but not before you go to bed.
- Write a to-do list for the following day and then clear your head of those concerns.
- Practice deep breathing or progressive muscle relaxation before bedtime.
- Avoid caffeine, alcohol, and nicotine, either entirely or at least in the evenings.
- Keep your bedroom at a cool temperature (65–68 degrees).
- If you are sensitive to light and sound, wear earplugs and a sleep mask or try a white noise machine to mask the sound. There are various white noise apps available if you have a smartphone.
- If you are having trouble falling asleep, get out of bed and do some light activity (like reading) in another room. Go back to bed when you feel drowsy.
- Go to bed and get up at the same time every day.
- Avoid eating heavy meals at least two to three hours before bed.
- Make sure your mattress and pillows are comfortable.
- Write down other ideas to help you get more sleep:

_____

_____

_____

Sleep Diary

Date	Hours Slept	Trouble Sleeping?	Methods Tried	Successful?
		☐ Y ☐ N		☐ Y ☐ N
		☐ Y ☐ N		☐ Y ☐ N
		☐ Y ☐ N		☐ Y ☐ N
		☐ Y ☐ N		☐ Y ☐ N
		☐ Y ☐ N		☐ Y ☐ N
		☐ Y ☐ N		☐ Y ☐ N
		☐ Y ☐ N		☐ Y ☐ N
		☐ Y ☐ N		☐ Y ☐ N
		☐ Y ☐ N		☐ Y ☐ N
		☐ Y ☐ N		☐ Y ☐ N
		☐ Y ☐ N		☐ Y ☐ N
		☐ Y ☐ N		☐ Y ☐ N
		☐ Y ☐ N		☐ Y ☐ N
		☐ Y ☐ N		☐ Y ☐ N
		☐ Y ☐ N		☐ Y ☐ N

Overcoming Anxiety with the Help of Exercise

Regular exercise can help you overcome your anxiety in a number of ways. During exercise, your brain increases the production of chemicals that can lift your mood and regulate your emotions. With regular exercise, you will feel stronger and more confident, and more likely to feel that you can make positive changes in your life. Exercise will also increase the oxygen flow to your brain, which may help you think more clearly and rationally and more positively.

Directions

1) Circle the types of exercise you can do on a regular basis:

bike riding	baseball	football	handball
jogging	hiking	soccer	karate
walking	skateboarding	surfing	Pilates
weight lifting	basketball	skiing	yoga
tennis	swimming	dancing	other

Write down any other exercises you think you can do that aren't listed above:

a) _____

b) _____

c) _____

d) _____

2) Now choose three of these exercises you would like to do over the next week.

a) _____

b) _____

c) _____

3) Decide how much time you need for each exercise. Fifteen minutes? A half-hour? An hour?

a)_____

b) _____

c) _____

4) For each of the exercises, write down how often you can realistically do them in a week.

a)_____

b) _____

c) _____

5) For each of the exercises, write down which days are best to exercise and what time of day is most realistic.

a)_____

b) _____

c) _____

Use this chart to record how many times you <u>actually</u> exercise and the effect that exercise has on your mood.

Day	Type of Exercise	Amount of Time	Mood Before	Mood Afterwards
Monday				
Tuesday				
Wednesday				
Thursday				
Friday				
Saturday				
Sunday				

How Diet Affects Your Mood

Diet, stress, and mood are all intertwined, so it's important to consider what you're putting in your body, not only for your physical health but also for your emotional well-being.

It is not necessary to go to extremes in changing your diet. By simply being more mindful of what you're putting in your body, you can find small ways to improve and that can add up to big changes.

The troublemakers …

- Caffeine: You'll find this stimulant in coffee, tea, chocolate, soda, energy drinks, and some over-the-counter medications. The temporary boost it provides can end in fatigue, headache, and tension. Caffeine has also been identified as a potential trigger for anxiety attacks and a contributor to other health issues such as insomnia, heartburn, aggression, irritability, heart palpitations, and high blood pressure.

- Salt: Sodium is present in many processed foods, so check labels and look for low-sodium or salt-free alternatives. Also, be aware of how much salt you use while cooking. Sodium consumption affects fluid retention, weight, and blood pressure, all of which, in turn, can affect your mood.

- Sugar: Excessive intake of simple sugars (such as white or brown sugar and honey) can cause health problems such as diabetes and hypoglycemia, the latter of which is often accompanied by symptoms similar to those experienced during a panic attack. Also, the temporary uplifting effects come with some other serious downsides, including an increased risk of depression in those who have a sugar-heavy diet.

- Preservatives and hormones: These substances are present in processed foods and many types of meats. Our bodies were not built to handle these additives, and their possible side effects have been heavily debated. Swapping in some whole, unprocessed, organic foods can help reduce consumption of these potentially harmful substances.

- Nicotine and alcohol: Introducing these substances into your system can cause a range of problems, not the least of which is aggravating anxiety. Nicotine is a stimulant, like caffeine, and alcohol a depressant. The addictive properties of both nicotine and alcohol have also been well documented.

It should also be mentioned that what you don't put in your body can also be problematic. Nutrient deficiencies and dehydration can cause irritability, anxiety, and fatigue. So stop skipping meals and make sure you are drinking enough water.

How Your Diet Affects Your Mood

For the next week, keep track of how often you consume any of the above-listed items, and write in the predominant moods you had each day.

Day	Food and Drink	Your Moods
Sunday		
Monday		
Tuesday		
Wednesday		
Thursday		
Friday		
Saturday		

Building Your Support System to Overcome Your Anxiety

People with anxiety disorders often find themselves isolated from others. They are often embarrassed about their problems and find it easier to just be alone rather than explain themselves to others. But avoiding people to avoid your anxiety will cause you two problems. You will miss many opportunities to enjoy your life which can only happen in the company of others and, by avoiding situations that cause you anxiety, you will likely prolong this psychological problem.

This worksheet can help you think about people who can support you in various areas of your life. If you have difficulty thinking of people in a specific area, think of people who could *possibly* fill this role, and then work towards making this happen. Often, you'll find you can get the support you need by just asking for it.

Write down at least one person you know who fits into each category.

Someone I can discuss a personal problem with:

_____

Phone: _____ Email: _____

Someone who enjoys similar activities:

_____

Phone: _____ Email: _____

Someone who can help me with a task:

_____

Phone: _____ Email: _____

Someone who can cheer me up when I am down:

_____

Phone: _____ Email: _____

Someone who builds my self-confidence:

_____

Phone: _____ Email: _____

Someone who can give me helpful feedback:

_____

Phone: _____ Email: _____

Someone who is a good listener and who is understanding:

_____

Phone: _____ Email: _____

Someone who can be honest with me when I'm making a mistake:

_____

Phone: _____ Email: _____

Someone who can keep me accountable for my decisions and goals:

_____

Phone: _____ Email: _____

Someone who can help me conquer bad habits:

_____

Phone: _____ Email: _____

Someone who can help me solve serious problems:

_____

Phone: _____ Email: _____

Someone I can count on to make me laugh:

_____

Phone: _____ Email: _____

Someone who can comfort me in a time of loss:

_____

Phone: _____ Email: _____

Someone who can care for me when I'm ill:

_____

Phone: _____ Email: _____

Someone who will be proud of my achievements and let me know it:

_____

Phone: _____ Email: _____

Someone else who can give me support:

Phone: _____ Email: _____

Someone else who can give me support:

Phone: _____ Email: _____

Someone else who can give me support:

Phone: _____ Email: _____

Someone else who can give me support:

Phone: _____ Email: _____

What Has Helped You?

Personal change can be a long and sometimes unexpected process. You can find solutions to your problems and conflicts from sudden insight or by following a carefully crafted plan. You can find help from working with your therapist and also from books, friends, and things you see on the Internet and social media, and much more.

Whatever your process in discovering solutions to your problems and conflicts, writing down what you have learned will be an important part of making lasting changes.

This worksheet is designed to help you think about what has helped you along your journey to overcome your problems. Take some time, at least once a month, to fill in the worksheet. You will likely find added benefit from sharing it with your therapist or a close friend. Of course, you can also use this worksheet more frequently. Using it more frequently may be helpful in times of stress and during difficult life transitions.

Today's date: _____

Specific skills I learned in therapy:

_____

_____

_____

Specific insights I have gotten from therapy:

_____

_____

_____

Books that have helped me (be specific about what has helped):

_____

_____

_____

Things that have inspired and motivated me (e.g., quotes, people, events, activities, etc.):

_____

_____

_____

Decisions I made that could help me with future choices:

_____

_____

_____

Spiritual practices or spiritual moments that have guided or inspired me:

_____

_____

_____

Changes in my habits that have made a difference:

_____

_____

_____

Other things that have helped me:

_____

_____

_____

After reflecting on what has helped you, what is the one thing you think made the most important positive impact?

_____

_____

Notes

Notes

Notes

CPSIA information can be obtained
at www.ICGtesting.com
Printed in the USA
LVOW09s1015180517

534996LV00016B/374/P

9 781947 009004